# Secrets
# of Success

ONE FOR EACH DAY OF THE MONTH

J. Donald Walters

CRYSTAL CLARITY
PUBLISHERS

14618 Tyler Foote Road
Nevada City, CA 95959

Cover and text design
by Julia B. Beinhorn

A SEED THOUGHT is offered for every day of the month. Begin a day at the appropriate date. Repeat the saying several times: first out loud, then softly, then in a whisper, and then only mentally. With each repetition, allow the words to become absorbed ever more deeply into your subconscious. Thus, gradually, you will acquire as complete an understanding as one might gain from a year's course in the subject. At this point, indeed, the truths set forth here will have become your own.

Keep the book open at the pertinent page throughout the day. Refer to it occasionally during moments of leisure. Relate the saying as often as possible to real situations in your life.

Then at night, before you go to bed, repeat the thought several times more. While falling asleep, carry the words into your subconscious, absorbing their positive influence into your whole being. Let it become thereby an integral part of your normal consciousness.

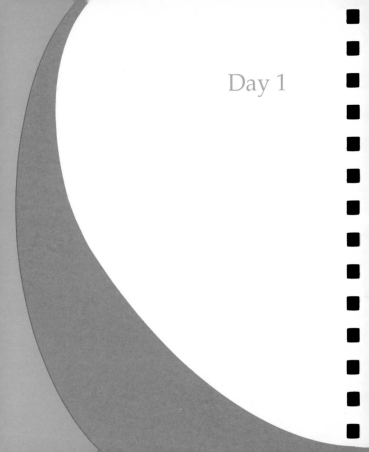

Day 1

The secret
of success is —

enjoying,
never bemoaning,
whatever effort
a work requires.

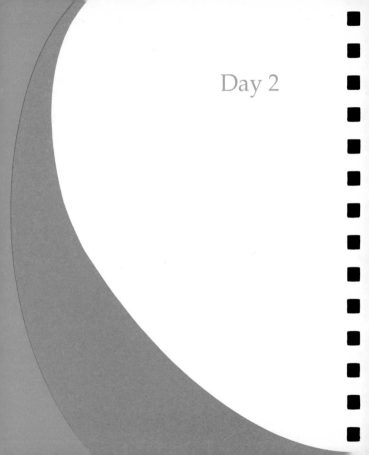

Day 2

The secret
   of success is —

doing things not merely
because they are popular,
but because you deeply
believe in them.

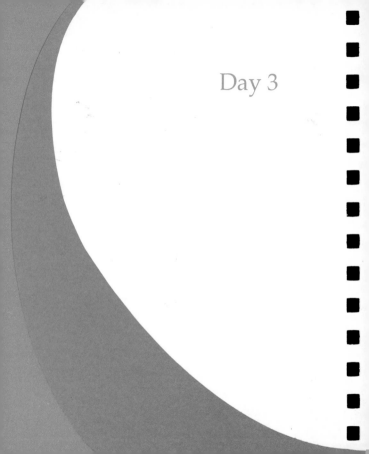

Day 3

The secret
of success is —

working with
things as they *are*,
not with the way
you wish they were
or think they ought to be.

Day 4

The secret
of success is —

non-attachment to results;
doing your best at the moment,
and letting the results
take care of themselves.

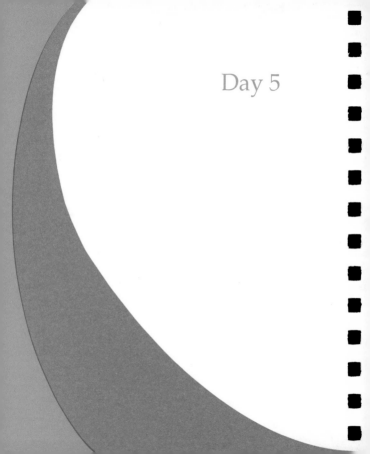

Day 5

The secret
of success is —

enthusiasm!
Without it,
nothing worthwhile
was ever achieved.

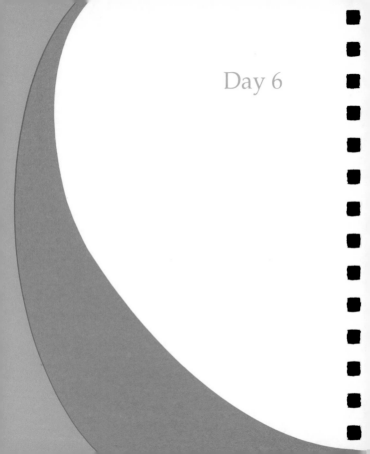

Day 6

The secret
of success is —

asking yourself always,
not, "What do I want
to see happen?" but rather,
"What is trying to happen here?"

Day 7

The secret
of success is —

seeing your work primarily
as a service to others,
and not as a means
of personal gain.

Day 8

The secret
of success is —

blaming no one
when things go wrong,
but doing whatever you can
to improve matters.

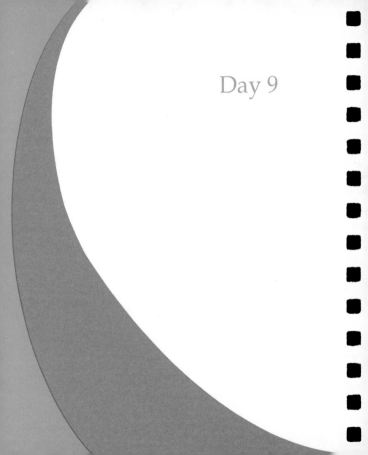

Day 9

The secret
of success is —

being crystal clear as to
your purpose and directions,
and having the courage
to act accordingly.

Day 10

The secret
of success is —

welcoming as opportunities
whatever obstacles
confront you.

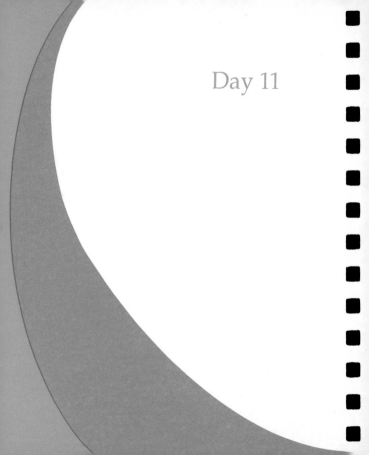

Day 11

The secret
of success is —

seeing every setback
as a steppingstone
to ultimate
achievement.

Day 12

The secret
of success is —

developing your will power,
by setting yourself increasingly
difficult goals, and persevering until
each of them has been achieved.

Day 13

The secret
of success is —

being more energy-oriented
than goal-oriented;
seeing life in terms of
constant progress, not of
pre-established ends.

Day 14

The secret
of success is —

daring to step outside
the boundaries of
conventional wisdom.

Day 15

The secret
of success is —

the ability to concentrate
one-pointedly on whatever task
you set yourself.

Day 16

The secret
of success is —

viewing every day as a fresh
beginning, bright with promise,
and never defining yourself
in terms of past accomplishments.

Day 17

The secret
of success is —

not limiting your self-identity
to present realities,
but expanding it to include
your highest potentials.

Day 18

The secret
of success is —

willingness to re-evaluate
your first principles.

Day 19

The secret
of success is —

ensuring that the outcome of
everything you do be harmonious,
by acting always with a positive,
harmonious attitude.

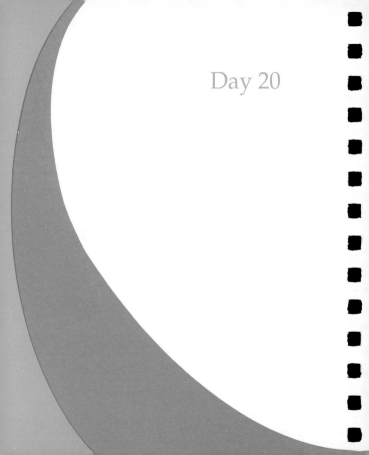

Day 20

The secret
of success is —

asking yourself in anything
you do, not merely, "What would
people like to have?" but,
"What would I feel happy
giving them?"

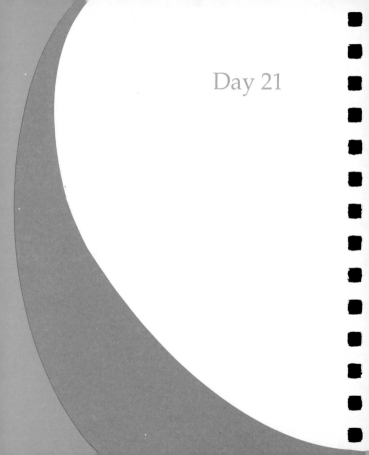

Day 21

The secret
   of success is —

openness to the truth,
no matter by whom
it is uttered.

Day 22

The secret
of success is —

a preference for the truth
over mere opinion —
even if the opinion
be your own.

Day 23

The secret
of success is —

consulting your inner feeling
before making decisions;
never doing a thing,
whatever Reason tells you,
unless your heart concurs.

Day 24

The secret
of success is —

never making emotional decisions,
but maintaining your heart's
feeling in a calm state of reason.

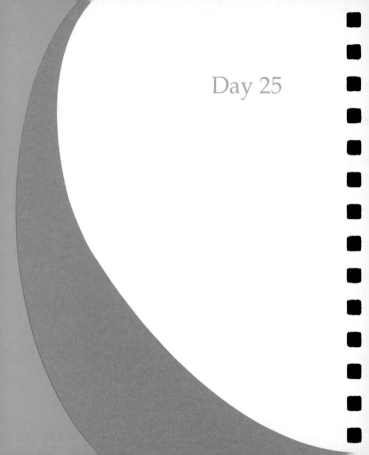

Day 25

The secret
of success is —

being solution-oriented,
not problem-oriented,
and having faith that,
for every problem,
an inherent solution exists.

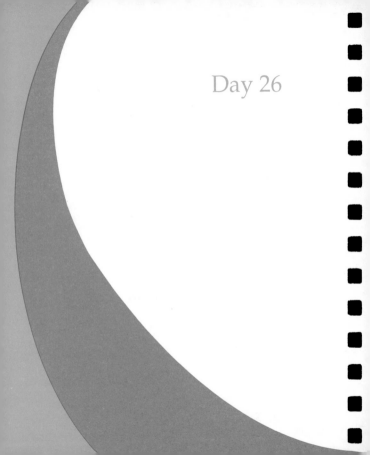

Day 26

The secret
of success is —

being grateful for
what you have, however little,
and not resenting life
for what it hasn't given you.

Day 27

The secret
of success is —

not making excuses for
yourself when things go
wrong, but reflecting that
God alone is infallible!

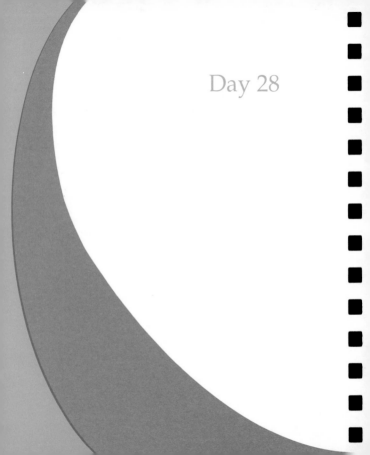

Day 28

The secret
of success is —

understanding that *you* are
the final measure of everything you
accomplish.  For that work alone
is noble which ennobles its creator.

Day 29

The secret
   of success is —


meeting challenges by
remaining calmly centered
within, and seeking strength
and guidance intuitively,
in your inner Self.

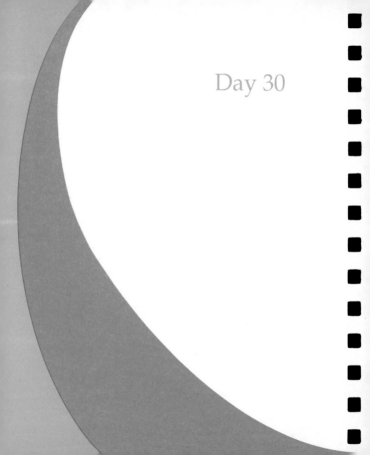

Day 30

The secret
of success is —

attuning your limited,
human will to the infinite
divine will.

Day 31

The secret
of success is —


humility;
realizing that pride
is the death of wisdom,
and the paralysis of every
worthwhile endeavor.

## Other Books
## by J. Donald Walters

For a brochure of these books and other selections
please write the publisher, or call 800-545-7475.